YOU CHOOSE
BOOKS

COULD YOU ESCAPE ALCATRAZ?

AN INTERACTIVE SURVIVAL ADVENTURE

BY ERIC BRAUN

CAPSTONE PRESS
a capstone imprint

You Choose Books are published by Capstone Press
1710 Roe Crest Drive, North Mankato, Minnesota 56003
www.capstonepub.com

Library of Congress Cataloging-in-Publication Data
Names: Braun, Eric, 1971– author.
Title: Could you escape Alcatraz? : an interactive survival adventure / by
  Eric Braun.
Description: North Mankato, Minnesota : Capstone Press, [2020] | Series: You
  choose: can you escape? | Summary: Cast as a prisoner in the infamous
  Alcatraz Penitentiary, the reader's choices determine if escape is
  possible.
Identifiers: LCCN 2019006018| ISBN 9781543573923 (hardcover) | ISBN
  9781543575613 (paperback) | ISBN 9781543573961 (ebook pdf)
Subjects: LCSH: Plot-your-own stories. | CYAC: Prisoners—Fiction. |
  Escapes—Fiction. | United States Penitentiary, Alcatraz Island,
  California—Fiction. | Plot-your-own stories.
Classification: LCC PZ7.1.B751542 Cou 2019 | DDC [Fic]—dc23
LC record available at https://lccn.loc.gov/2019006018

Editorial Credits
Mari Bolte, editor; Bobbie Nuytten, designer; Eric Gohl, media researcher:
Laura Manthe, premedia specialist

Photo Credits
AP Photo: Clarence Hamm, 72, Ernest K. Bennett, 99; Eric Gohl: 37, 42, 94, 105;
Getty Images: Anadolu Agency, 24, Bettmann, 21, 91; Library of Congress: 66, 77,
87; Newscom: Everett Collection, 4, 6; Shutterstock: Arne Beruldsen, 63, brian takes
photos, 51, Clari Massimiliano, 29, kenkistler, 83, Milan Sommer, 47, MintImages, 34,
Nick Heinimann, 10, PeanutsNSoda, cover, back cover, superjoseph, 102; Wikimedia:
NPS, 17, 56

All internet sites appearing in back matter were available and accurate when this book
was sent to press.

Printed and bound in the United States of America.
PA70

TABLE OF CONTENTS

Map Key:

1 maintenance shop

2 power house

3 prison yard

4 hall and kitchen

5 main cell block

6 administration and warden's office

7 dock

8 guard recreation yard

9 catwalk

10 guard tower

ABOUT YOUR ADVENTURE

YOU are about to become a prisoner at the infamous Alcatraz Federal Penitentiary. Nicknamed "The Rock", it is famous for keeping dangerous prisoners from escaping. But that won't stop you from trying.

Start the story. Then follow the directions at the bottom of each page. You may have done wrong in the past, but the choices you make will change the outcome. After you finish one path, go back and read the others to see how the decisions you make change your fate. Do you have what it takes to make it off The Rock?

Turn the page to begin your adventure.

Chapter 1

A HARD LIFE ON THE ROCK

You're here—the famous Alcatraz Island. The prison sits 1.25 miles (2.4 kilometers) away from the mainland of San Francisco. That's a long swim to freedom.

To get here, you were delivered by boat across cold, choppy water. You and other prisoners were shackled and watched closely by armed guards. When the boat docked, you looked up at the prison—high walls made of stone and brick, and topped with barbed wire. Frigid wind tussled your hair and chilled your skin.

As you stepped onto the island, you were searched and given a prison uniform. Then you were assigned to a cell.

Turn the page.

All this time, you looked carefully around you, noting every detail of your surroundings. How high the fence was, how long the hallway, how thick the iron bars. Already thinking of escape. Could it be done?

Everyone says Alcatraz is inescapable. Now that you've been here a while, you have to admit, it just might be. Even if you were to somehow get out of your cell, out of the building, over the walls, past the machine gun towers, and across the bay to the mainland, then what? You would be cold, wet, without money or transportation . . . and you'd be wearing a prison uniform. Blending in would be a real problem. Where would you go after that?

But here's an even bigger problem: Life on The Rock is hard. It's boring, harsh, and often violent. Meanwhile, a life of freedom teases you like the sunshine that occasionally peeks over the high prison yard walls.

Maybe no one has escaped The Rock before. Maybe you won't be able to either. But you have to give it a shot. Success will depend on the person you choose to be. Pick wisely!

To be an athlete with great strength and endurance, turn to page 11.

To be a highly intelligent criminal mastermind, turn to page 43.

To be a mechanic who can build anything, turn to page 73.

Chapter 2

THE ATHLETE PLAYS FOR KEEPS

You were a star athlete in high school. In football, you were a running back, fast and bruising. In baseball, you played first base and hit home runs. Maybe most important of all, you were a record-setting swimmer. You were happy.

But then your father died. You had no choice but to drop out of school to take a job. You had to help pay rent and buy food for you, your little brother, and mom. You worked your fingers to the bone at an auto plant.

Even with your job, money was tight. To make ends meet, you started to steal from stores. Soon you graduated to robbing people, then to robbing banks. You got away with it for a while.

Turn the page.

But then your luck ran out. Eventually you were caught and sent to prison. When you got out, you went right back to robbing. What else could you do? Your family was desperate.

The second time you went to prison, you overpowered a guard while working in a field. You hid in the woods for three days before being caught. The judge sent you to The Rock so you couldn't escape again.

Now you lie on your cot at night and remember your days as a sports star. You miss those old, simpler times.

You also worry about your family. You would love to see your mom and brother again. And so you plan your escape. The way you see it, there are two ways to do it.

To rely on your strength and speed, go to page 13.
To take a more sneaky approach, turn to page 15.

Your athletic abilities are your greatest tools. You might as well use them.

You're not thrilled with the idea of using violence, but you're sure it's your best chance. If you don't escape, you will be killed in a fight or sent to solitary—a small, pitch-black cell all by yourself. Solitary can drive a person insane. Just the threat is enough to keep most men from trying to escape.

You will need help to pull this off. After dinner one night, a guard passes your cell, making his rounds. When he's out of earshot, you step up to the front corner of your cell and whisper to the man in the next cell over. Hanson is not strong like you, but he's been on The Rock a long time. He knows its secrets. He's also your friend. You trust him.

Turn the page.

"Hanson," you whisper. "Let's see the moon."

This is code for getting out. Nobody in Alcatraz ever sees the moon because they're locked up at night.

Hanson is silent a moment. Perhaps he is stunned by your proposal. Then comes his barely audible reply: "Yes."

Over the next few nights, you talk at the front of your cells, making a plan. Hanson has a job in the maintenance shop in the Model Industries building and says only two guards are on duty on weekends.

To try to get a job in maintenance with Hanson, turn to page 16.

To have Hanson steal a weapon from the shop, turn to page 18.

Fighting and running can only end in disaster. You'll have better luck if you can find a way to sneak out.

Not long after you make this decision, you are assigned a job in the kitchen. Every day you help unload groceries that are delivered on a boat. Wooden crates of meat. Sacks of flour and rice. Big plastic racks of milk jugs. Boxes of canned goods. It's not the most interesting job in the world, but it's a change of pace.

Twice a week, bags of bread arrive at the kitchen inside a huge wooden crate. As you unload bread from the box one day, you realize that it is just big enough to fit a person inside if you sit with your knees tight to your chest. These bread crates could be the key to your escape.

To try to escape inside a bread box, turn to page 20.
To wait for another, more complete plan, turn to page 23.

Within a couple weeks, Hanson is able to get you a job in the maintenance shop. You work side-by-side with a couple other prisoners. Just like Hanson said, two guards work on weekends. As long as you stay focused on your job and don't cause any trouble, the guards leave you alone.

The only windows in the maintenance shop are reinforced with heavy steel bars. But if you can get through the bars, you'll be outside the prison walls and right next to the sea. The Model Industries building is at the northernmost point of the island. It might be a while before you're missed.

Hanson tells you of an old rumor: a convict once stole a life jacket and hid it in the bushes down the beach from the maintenance shop. He is confident that it's still there. If you make it to the water, you can take turns resting on the life jacket and float to safety.

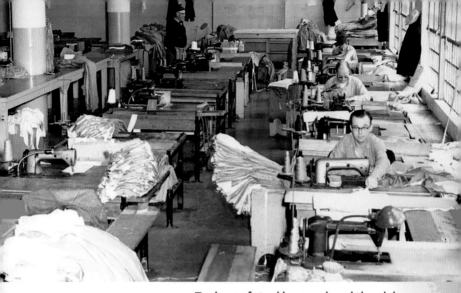

Tool-proof steel bars replaced the plain metal bars over the windows in 1934.

Should you let the other two prisoners in on the plot? Can you trust them? Maybe they can help. Ramstad is a big man, and he could help in many ways. Kelly is a cold-blooded murderer. A guy like that could be useful—or turn on you.

No matter what, you *have* to tell them something. They will be in the room when you attack the guards. You need them ready.

To invite Ramstad and Kelly to join you, turn to page 26.

To ask for their help, turn to page 27.

Hanson can't get metal through the metal detector at the shop, so he steals a block of wood. At dinner one night, he talks to his friend Stinky about a saw blade that he hid long ago when he worked in the laundry room. Stinky is on the side of anyone who might escape. He agrees to retrieve the blade.

It arrives hidden in a bundle of clean sheets at Hanson's cell. That night after lights-out, Hanson wraps one end of the blade in a towel to make a handle and saws the hunk of wood into a dagger.

Later, he sneaks another block of wood and the saw blade to you. Now it's your turn to fashion a dagger. You have a close call that night when you drop the metal saw. It clangs on the concrete floor. You quickly hide the blade and wooden dagger behind some books on your shelf and get in bed.

The guard comes to your cell and shines his light inside. You squint up at him and act as if he just woke you. You try to look sleepy, but inside your heart is racing.

Thankfully, the guard casts his light around your cell and walks past.

Will he tell the other guards about the metallic sound? Will they be watching you?

To plan your escape for as soon as possible, turn to page 29.
To wait until the heat dies down, turn to page 31.

You enlist two trusted friends in the kitchen to help you. Late one afternoon, an inmate named Stinky starts a fight with another inmate in the kitchen. This is all part of the plan. When the guards go to break it up, you quickly climb into the box, and your friend clasps it shut.

You feel yourself being lifted gracefully, and then you are on the move. Before long you smell the salty ocean air, and your heart fills with excitement. You're outside!

Then you hear a voice calling. It's Lieutenant French, one of the guards.

"Hold it!" he says. "Why does that empty box look so heavy? Open it up."

You feel the box clunk on the dock. Outside, your friend Ginger Mac says, "It ain't heavy, what're you talking about?"

Footsteps approach the box. You do not allow yourself a breath.

"You want me to open it up?" Ginger Mac says. "It's empty." He starts to undo one of the clasps.

But French says, "Just load it up."

You feel yourself lifted once again. Next time you come down, you know you are inside the cargo bay of a boat. Soon, the boat leaves the dock.

Turn the page.

A guard tower overlooks the pier where visitors tie up their boats.

Once your shift in the kitchen is over, they will do a count and realize you're missing. You don't have much time. So you kick open the box and creep to the front of the cargo bay. Sea air whips all around you.

You dive over the railing and plunge into the cold water.

It's dark outside by the time the patrol boats are out. They sweep their searchlights across the surface. You swim underwater as much as you can. You make it to land and crawl up a rocky beach, panting and cold. You hide in a cliff opening.

The next morning you hear helicopters in the air. And you hear dogs patrolling the beach. You realize it's only a matter of time before you're caught.

THE END

To follow another path, turn to page 9.
To learn more about Alcatraz, turn to page 103.

Sneaking out of prison in a bread box? It's just too ridiculous. It would never work.

Instead, you spend the next few weeks playing chess with some of the other inmates in the yard during outdoor time. You manage to make friends with Papa, a powerful gangster. One day, over a game of chess, you tell Papa about your desire to escape. You ask for his advice.

He looks up at the squawking seagulls for a few seconds. Then he says, very quietly, "Let me talk to someone."

Four days later, you are playing chess with Papa again. He takes your rook with his queen. "Check," he says. Then, quieter, he says, "Get real sick. Sickest you've ever been. There's a bar spreader taped under the second bed in the infirmary."

Turn the page.

A day later you're in your cell eating an old, dead rat that you found and stashed. Its body is crawling with insects and decay.

At dinner that night you become violently ill and are carried to the infirmary. Someone takes your vital signs and hooks you up to an IV. You keep retching. You hope you're not actually too sick to make your escape.

According to Alcatraz regulations, prisoners were entitled to food, clothing, shelter, and medical attention.

Later, loud noises echo from the hallway. You remember that Papa promised a distraction. The guard leaves to check it out. You pull out the IV and reach for the bar spreader—basically a long rod. You use it to knock out the nurse.

You lock the door, climb on top of the bed, and open the window. You pry the bars behind the window apart.

You dash into the ocean. It's freezing. *You're strong*, you remind yourself. But as you push your body to its limits, you throw up. Your head starts to spin.

You realize you are too weak to make this trip. You will drown if you continue. You have to swim back and turn yourself in.

THE END

To follow another path, turn to page 9.
To learn more about Alcatraz, turn to page 103.

Those two prisoners are not going to solitary to help you, that's for sure. The smart thing to do would be to invite them along. Hanson runs a grinder to cover his voice while he tells them your plan. Ramstad and Kelly tell Hanson they want to talk about it. They'll let you know tomorrow.

Something about the exchange doesn't sit right with you. Why would they have to talk it over? They might be planning to turn you in.

That night you and Hanson gather at the corners of your adjoining cells. You whisper, "I don't like it."

"They're solid," Hanson says back. He means you can trust them.

"It doesn't feel right," you say.

If you trust Kelly and Ramstad, turn to page 33.
If you decide to make a new plan, turn to page 36.

Most men on The Rock would love to see it "broken"—to see someone escape. You figure that includes Kelly and Ramstad. So Hanson lets them in on your plan. He asks them to keep the guards tied up while you get as far as you can.

"So we just stay here while you get away?" Ramstad says. He runs the drill press as he speaks, and the noise covers your conversation.

"This puts us in a bad spot," Kelly adds.

"I'm up for parole next year," Ramstad says, frowning. If he helps you, he'll never get parole.

You'll have to think of another way. But the next day, your cell is "tossed." The warden and two guards come and search it thoroughly. They turn over your mattress. They check between the pages of your books. They look under your sink. They even squirt out your toothpaste.

Turn the page.

They find nothing. They question you, but you tell them nothing.

You know that Ramstad ratted you out. Helping the guys in charge will show that he's a changed man. This will strengthen his case for parole. You wish there was a way to get revenge on him before he gets out, but there isn't. You just have to watch him go free and keep waiting for your own chance.

THE END

To follow another path, turn to page 9.
To learn more about Alcatraz, turn to page 103.

The next day, you and Hanson hide your wooden daggers inside your jackets. He has gotten approval to have you help him in the maintenance shop for the day. You plan to stab your guard on the way there. Then you should be able to get over the fence and into the water before anyone knows you're missing.

Turn the page.

The fences around Alcatraz were 12 feet (3.7 meters) high and topped with barbed wire and razor wire.

The plan seems pretty solid. As a state champion swimmer, you know that you'll be able to make it all the way to shore. As for Hanson, who knows?

Unfortunately, you don't get a chance to try your plan. You were right about heat being on you. When the guards come to your cell, they tell you to leave your jacket and shoes in the cell. Then more guards come—and so does the warden. You know this is not good news.

As you watch, the guards "toss," or search, your cell. They find the saw blade in a book and the dagger in your jacket. Hanson gets searched too. You and Hanson exchange a sad look before the guards lead you to solitary confinement.

THE END

To follow another path, turn to page 9.
To learn more about Alcatraz, turn to page 103.

If the guard tells anyone what he heard, you could be in trouble. Nervous, you call off the escape attempt.

Two days later, you learn that you were right: They *were* onto you. While you are in the mess hall, the warden and two guards come into your cell and search it. They find the weapon and the saw blade. And, knowing that you are friends with Hanson, they also search his cell. They find his dagger as well.

You are sent to solitary. It is dark, lonely, and silent. The cell is tiny. You have to fight every day to keep your wits—it feels like you're going insane. You've always been strong physically. Mental toughness is a different thing. How long have you been here? You've lost track.

Turn the page.

Wait—was that a voice? It can't be. Nobody is here. But in the dark you can't be sure.

It *was* a voice. You're sure of it. Kind of.

It's your mother. Can that be right? It sounds like her. She scolds you for robbing those people. She didn't raise you like that. You knew it was wrong. What were you thinking?

She loves you though. She misses you. It's nice to hear her voice.

THE END

To follow another path, turn to page 9.
To learn more about Alcatraz, turn to page 103.

You hear from Kelly and Ramstad soon enough: They're in.

And the news is even better than you hoped. Ramstad has a girlfriend in San Francisco. She will hide you—if you can get there.

Early in your shift the next day, Kelly strikes one guard across the face with a wrench. Hanson and Ramstad beat the other with their hands while you take a long metal file to the window. The other three tie up the bleeding guards with an electrical cord.

"Hurry, hurry," Kelly mutters at you. You work as fast as you can, your hands getting shredded as you go. When you get through the bar, you use the wrench to pry the bar away from the window.

Turn the page.

Outside, Hanson finds the hidden life jacket. The four of you wade into the water, then swim as fast as you can. You trade off holding onto the life jacket so you each get short rests. Still, the trip is exhausting. At least the waves are mild.

The water around Alcatraz is usually very cold, around 60 degrees Fahrenheit (15.5 degrees Celsius).

You wash up on a beach and walk north for nearly a mile along the jagged coast. You pass a group of seals sunning on some big rocks. You imagine the authorities will be searching for you now.

Finally, you reach a set of stairs. At the top, sitting in a blue pickup truck, is Ramstad's girlfriend. You lay in the truck bed out of sight until you reach her apartment.

Once there, the woman heats up a couple cans of soup. You've made it! At least for now. You try to relax, but every sound makes you jump. For the rest of your life you'll be looking over your shoulder. But for now, you eat your soup and enjoy being free.

THE END

To follow another path, turn to page 9.
To learn more about Alcatraz, turn to page 103.

You don't know Kelly and Ramstad very well. It's not worth the risk. You let them know the escape is off. Now, you wait.

It is months before you get another chance. You put in a transfer out of maintenance and onto the garbage crew. You and Hanson devise a plan to get transported out of the prison with the garbage. When the load is dumped at the loading dock, you tumble out with the garbage. Hanson breaks his arm in the fall. It smells so awful that Hanson throws up on himself. You just tell him to keep the noise down.

After dark, you climb out of the garbage into the water. But you're only a few hundred yards out into the ocean before Hanson starts to struggle. He wasn't a very strong guy to begin with. With the broken arm, he's even weaker.

The water currents around the island are strong and unpredicatable.

"Float on your back," you call to him. You put an arm around his chest and pull him toward you. You sidestroke toward the mainland, dragging Hanson with you. But before long, you start to get tired too.

To let him go, turn to page 38.
To keep helping him, turn to page 40.

You realize you have no choice if you want to live. You can either let him slip into the water and drown, giving yourself a chance to survive, or you hold on—and drown with him.

"I'm sorry!" you yell as you release him. Suddenly he has more energy than he did before. He grasps and claws at you with his good arm. Terror fills his eyes. "I'm sorry!" you say again. It is a terrible moment. But it only takes a few seconds for you to get away. He doesn't say any last words, just disappears in the dark waves.

You turn toward the mainland and swim harder. Your strokes are smooth and efficient. At the beach, you find a small parking lot. It's empty except for one car. Inside, a man and woman are sitting arm in arm.

You grab a large rock off the beach and run toward the driver's door. You pull the door open and pull him out. He's about your size. You lift the rock high.

"Take off your clothes!" you yell.

He does. The sweater is a little tight across your broad chest and you can't button the pants, but it will do. You leave the two of them in the parking lot and drive away in their car.

As you drive, you try to decide where to go. Maybe there's a map in the glove compartment. And you'll need to fill the car's tank eventually. The important thing for now, though, is to just keep going.

THE END

To follow another path, turn to page 9.
To learn more about Alcatraz, turn to page 103.

It might be hopeless, but you just can't leave your friend to drown. So despite feeling tired, you keep on pulling him through the water. Slowly, you make your way across the bay. The sun comes up. You see that you are still several hundred yards from shore.

A sharp cramp develops in your left hamstring. It's so deep and painful, you actually scream. You can't move your leg, and for a second you taste seawater in your mouth. You're slipping. Furiously, you pump your other leg and your free arm and get above water again. You take deep breaths. Hanson is kicking too, but it's not much help. You taste the water again.

Just rest a second, you think.

And you relax. Your two bodies float for a moment, then start going down. You let them. The rest helps. You can feel strength trickle back into your limbs. You kick again, and you rise to the surface. Your teeth are chattering. Your look at your fingers—they're blue.

You sink again.

You pump your legs, but it's not enough. You sink. And sink.

You can't feel anything.

THE END

To follow another path, turn to page 9.
To learn more about Alcatraz, turn to page 103.

Chapter 3

THE MASTERMIND STRIKES AGAIN

You have made a career out of escaping from prisons. You've taken an early vacation from three others before this. You don't think Alcatraz will be any different.

The first time, you were just 16. You stole a car for fun and got sent to county jail. You escaped by distracting the guard at dinner. Then you hit him over the head with his own gun.

You stayed out of trouble for a while, but at age 20 you were caught in an armed robbery. This time you were sent to federal prison in Kansas. There, your cellmate was an older guy who recognized your intelligence and keen skills.

Turn the page.

Clancy helped you better understand how to case a prison and figure out escape routes. He taught you how to time the guards on their rounds, watch them interact, and learn which ones aren't too smart. He told you how to figure out which ones have a big ego that you can use to your advantage. You should make friends with the old-timers so you can learn their secrets. He even taught you about prison architecture.

You escaped that prison within the year. But you were caught robbing a store a couple years later, returning to prison once again. This time you escaped and lived in hiding for years, fooling the authorities. When they finally caught you, the arresting agent advised the judge to send you to a place where escape would be impossible. That meant one thing: You went to The Rock.

"I guarantee you won't escape *that!*" the judge said.

You took it as a challenge.

You haven't been here long when another prisoner recognizes you. Kelly approaches you in the yard and tells you he was in that Kansas prison when you broke out. "I know a way out of here," he says. He wants to team up with you to escape from Alcatraz.

To team up with Kelly, turn to page 46.
To go it alone, turn to page 48.

It's cold in the yard today, and Kelly isn't wearing his jacket. Tough guy. Yeah, you remember him.

"All right," you say. You glance around to make sure nobody is listening. "What's this big secret you have?"

"Buddy of mine worked in maintenance some years ago," Kelly says. "He took a fan out of a ceiling shaft above our cell block. He was supposed to repair it and put it back. But you know how things go—he got pulled off on another job. That fan never went back in."

"So the shaft is open," you say.

"All we have to do is get up there. From there, we can get on the roof."

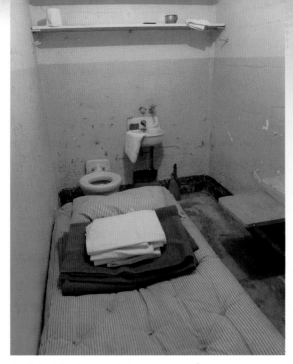

Cells in Blocks B and C were 5 by 9 feet
(1.5 by 2.7 m).

That night, you stare at the ceiling in your cell and imagine the open shaft. How can you get up there? You can study the guards for a couple weeks and try to figure out their patterns. Maybe they'll give you a clue. On the other hand, maybe there's a way to dig out of your cell.

To study the guards, turn to page 50.
To dig your way out, turn to page 53.

You never know who you can trust, especially in prison. You're already uncomfortable with the attention from Kelly. The guards notice every friendship, every suspicious activity . . . every move you make.

"Sorry," you tell Kelly, "I'm not looking for trouble right now."

Over the next few weeks, you case every inch of the prison. You watch the guards during mealtime. You study the bathroom and shower. In the yard, you scan the guard towers, gates, and wall. You watch the mail delivery, laundry collection, trash cleanup, and headcount procedures.

You are assigned a job in the laundry room. The big machines fill the air with hot steam. The smell of cleaning chemicals is strong.

Many convicts use the laundry to pass messages and illegal items. You quickly learn who has power in Alcatraz. And one person seems to have a lot of friends—and a lot of secrets. That person is Kelly.

You're learning a lot. But so far, you haven't found any way to get out.

"OK," you tell Kelly one night. "I give up. What's your secret?"

Kelly tells you about an open air shaft behind the walls of your cells. It leads to the maintenance corridor above the cell block. If you can get to the air shaft, you can use it to climb to freedom. What will you do?

To join forces with Kelly, turn to page 53.
To keep trying on your own, turn to page 55.

Every day, every waking moment, you keep one eye on the guards around you. When they change shifts, you listen to what they say. When they pass your cell, you notice what they're looking at. You check which ones are armed with guns and which are not.

One night after lights out, Lieutenant French pauses in front of your cell and looks in at you. You're lying on the bed trying to ignore him, but he doesn't leave.

"You need something?" you say.

Finally he speaks up. "You're not so bright, you know."

"What?" you say, stunned.

"I see what you're doing. And I'm telling you: I will be ready."

Then he takes a metal baton and raps on each of the bars of your cell. He's listening for any bar that might produce a flatter sound—evidence that it has been tampered with. But all the bars ring true. In the darkness, you see a tiny hint of a smile on his face.

Turn the page.

At its height, Alcatraz housed 302 prisoners.

"Good night," he says.

Your skin turns cold. You think back and realize that French has been watching you as much as you've been watching him. Your reputation as an escape artist has worked against you. French is smart. You almost respect him. If you met on the outside, you might even be friends.

The guard's footsteps echo down the cell block. His baton raps against more bars. You lie in the dark and listen. It sinks in that you can't risk an escape. Not while Lieutenant French is here. And he's going to be here a long time.

THE END

To follow another path, turn to page 9.
To learn more about Alcatraz, turn to page 103.

You tell Kelly that you think there's a way to dig out of the cells. But you need a good tool. Then you sit and wait patiently for something to happen.

One day in the yard, Kelly slips you something wrapped in cloth. Back in your cell, you carefully open it up. It's a drill bit. He really is well-connected.

That night, you use the drill bit to scrape around the air vent under your sink. The vent leads to the air shaft. Chunks of concrete start falling off. Each night you work for a couple hours while Kelly keeps a lookout. When a guard enters the cell block, Kelly gives two quick taps on the bars of his cell. That's your signal to move clothes in front of the grate and get quickly into bed.

Turn the page.

Before long, you have chipped all the way through the wall in a rectangle around the grate. You can pull it out. You give Kelly the drill bit to work on his own vent.

While you're waiting for him to chip around his vent, you decide you should go up and investigate that air shaft. The only problem is, the guards check the cells every hour. Can you crawl through the opening in your cell, climb up the maintenance corridor, find the open air shaft, inspect it, and get back to your cell before the guards come around again?

If you believe you can do it, turn to page 58.
To try to come up with a safer way, turn to page 60.

You can't trust anyone, not even Kelly. Besides, you have a plan. From your job in the laundry, you can steal a guard uniform one piece at a time. Once you have it all together, you can wait for the right time during your shift to slip out. Your uniform will get you onto a ferry back to the mainland.

After watching the guards for weeks, you pick your target. The one named Giles is not very bright. You've seen him forget to lock a gate, miscount prisoners on shift, and get confused about where he was supposed to be. Other guards make fun of him. Lieutenant French picks on him. He could be an easy target.

You hide the uniform behind a stack of bleach barrels. Once you have it ready, it's time to make your move on Giles. You start by letting him know you have noticed how Lieutenant French treats him.

Turn the page.

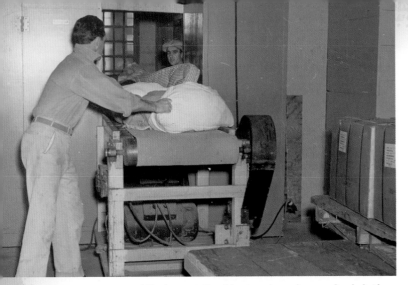

Workers at the Alcatraz laundry washed clothes for military bases in the San Francisco Bay area.

"I thought you ordered the cleanout line cleared today," you say one afternoon. "I guess French overruled you again."

Another day you mention how the big laundry carts need repairs. Several of the wheels are going bad. "Didn't you tell French about it?"

"I told him," Giles says. "He says to wait. He thinks he's smarter than everyone."

"He ought to listen to you more," you say.

It takes months, but Giles starts to think of you as an ally. Finally, you take a chance and ask Giles to make a copy of the gate key. You'll escape in your stolen uniform while French is on duty. It will make French look bad. Maybe he'll even be fired.

The laundry machines hum and clank while Giles chews his cheek, thinking. Does he hate French enough to frame him?

"Lieutenant French *is* a jerk," he says. "But I can't do that. I'll tell you what I *will* do, though. I'll wait until tomorrow to search the supply area. You might want to make sure I don't find anything."

Well, you think, *There's no getting off The Rock today*. But at least your friendship with Giles saved you from solitary.

THE END

To follow another path, turn to page 9.
To learn more about Alcatraz, turn to page 103.

It shouldn't be hard to get up there and back in less than an hour. All you are doing is checking to see if the shaft really is open and how big it is.

After the guard passes through the cell block, you jump out of bed. As quietly as possible, you slide out the grate. You shimmy through the narrow opening one shoulder at a time. Then you reach back into the cell and pull the grate back in place.

You feel your way in the dark until you find a set of pipes, and you begin to climb up. At the top of the third floor cell block, you step onto the landing. Craning your neck to peer up, you scan the ceiling shafts. They're all dark and full. But then through one shaft you see a cloudy moonlit sky. Jackpot!

Time is running short, so you quickly descend the pipes. When you push your cell vent out of the way, it clatters onto the floor. The sound echoes in the cell block.

Just as you are hurrying to climb back into your cell, a light shines in your eyes. "What's going on here?" the guard says. You close your eyes and picture that open shaft. That memory is as close as you'll ever get to seeing the night sky again.

THE END

To follow another path, turn to page 9.
To learn more about Alcatraz, turn to page 103.

Right now there is something more important than sneaking out. You have to hide the dug-out concrete around the grate in your cell. You've been keeping clothes in front of it, but it won't be long before the guards get suspicious.

At dinner one night, you lean close and whisper to Kelly, "Start requesting magazines from the library. Lots of them." Your plan is to tear out pages from the magazines, cut the pages into strips, and mix them with glue and concrete dust to make paper-mache. From that, you can make a fake model of the concrete and grate.

"You're a genius," Kelly says.

You also order painting supplies. Since you both have good behavior records, you're allowed to paint pictures in your cell. Of course, you have other plans for the paint.

You mix the paper-mache in your sink and build a fake vent grate. You paint it to match the mint green wall of your cell. You remove the real grate and slide it into the maintenance corridor behind your cell. The fake one fits perfectly. Next, you make paper-mache dummy heads and paint them to look like your and Kelly's heads.

The final step is to find a way to get off the island. Through your job in the laundry, you learn that an inmate named Papa is a powerful gangster. He has connections on the outside. People say he can make things happen.

But is it smart to get another person involved in your plan?

To ask Papa for help, turn to page 62.
To find your own way with Kelly, turn to page 65.

Wide concrete steps runs along one side of the exercise yard. Inmates call them the "bleachers." The longer you have been inside, and the more powerful you are, the higher you are allowed to sit. Nobody would dare climb too high up the bleachers—not unless they wanted to get killed.

Papa sits at the very top. One cool spring day you ask for permission to come up.

You do have a bit of a friendship with Papa. You have passed contraband for him in the laundry. Still, you are nervous until Papa's messenger comes down and says it's okay.

You climb the bleachers and thank the gangster for letting you up. You tell him your situation: You have a way to get out, but you need help. You describe the plan. You assure Papa that you have been extremely careful. It will work.

Prisoners spent as little as an hour
a week in the prison yard.

Papa agrees. You have proved yourself to be cunning and trustworthy. He says he can get a boat into the water outside the prison. You have to be ready when he gives the word.

More than a month passes. Then suddenly you get the word: Tonight is the night!

Turn the page.

Anxious, you lay in bed while the guard does his first count of the evening. After he leaves the cell block, you place your dummy head on the pillow and stuff clothes under the blanket. You slip into the maintenance corridor and replace the paper grate.

Next door, Kelly is still finishing digging out his grate. Unlike you, he hasn't gotten out yet. And there's a problem: An extra bar reinforces the concrete around his vent.

To help Kelly get his grate out, turn to page 68.
To go without him, turn to page 70.

One night while cutting ads out of a sporting magazine, an article catches your eye. It is about body surfing. It gives you an idea. A supply boat ferries back to the mainland every night. You can body surf behind it and get to the coast.

Kelly steals a long coil of rope from the maintenance shop. You both place your dummy heads on your pillows after lights out, slip out of your cells, and climb through the open air vent onto the roof.

Though it is foggy, you can see the moon flash through moving clouds. It has been a long time since you have been outside at night. The sight thrills you.

There's no time to admire the view, though. You and Kelly climb down to the dock. Workers are loading the supply boat. You wait.

Turn the page.

When the boat is loaded, you slip under the dock and toss your rope over the ship's railing. Kelly grabs the other end. As the boat pulls away, you both lean forward. You skim along the surface behind the boat.

There are nearly a dozen species of sharks in the San Francisco Bay, including Great Whites.

As you near the mainland, you release the rope and swim into a cove. On the road above, you walk until you find an unlocked car parked in an apartment parking lot.

The first hint of dawn sets the parking lot aglow. You feel a thrill of freedom as you hotwire the car. That's when you hear tires on the pavement.

"Get down!" Kelly whispers. "It's a cop!"

But it's too late. The police car's red and blue lights flash on, and a voice comes over a loud speaker: "Get out and put your hands up!"

It looks like you are going back to The Rock.

THE END

To follow another path, turn to page 9.
To learn more about Alcatraz, turn to page 103.

The smart thing to do is leave. You know this. But your emotions get the better of you. You can't bring yourself to ditch Kelly.

You wrap your hand around the exposed bar. You pull with all your strength, and it bends toward you. You push it back toward Kelly, then pull it back toward you. You repeat this several times, your hands blistering. Do it enough times, and the bar will snap. But how many times?

You rest while Kelly takes over bending the bar back and forth. He grunts and curses, and you whisper at him to shut up. When a guard passes for the hourly count, Kelly gets back in bed. You hold your breath as the guard passes your dummy head. It fools him. He doesn't give it a second look.

Finally you decide you have to go. The boat will not wait all night. "I'm sorry," you tell him. The look on Kelly's face is enough to make you hesitate. But you really have to go.

You slip easily outside and swim out into the dark water. You've lost at least an hour helping Kelly, and you hope the boat will still be there. You swim toward where it is supposed to be.

You swim farther. You're shivering. You should have seen the boat by now. Gradually it sinks in that it has left. You missed your chance.

THE END

To follow another path, turn to page 9.
To learn more about Alcatraz, turn to page 103.

That boat will not wait long for you. You need to go—now.

"I'll tell them to wait for you," you say to Kelly. But you both know this is a lie. As you climb the pipes toward the top of the building, you hear Kelly crying in his cell. It feels crushing. But you have no choice. If you want to get away, you have to be selfish.

Once outside, a guard tower sweeps its powerful search light along the beach. You lay in some brush and hide the best you can. The light moves smoothly past.

You don't have to swim very far before you see a small blue light flicker three times. That's the signal. You call out, and a motor croaks to life in the black night. It draws near, and a man reaches down to pull you out of the water.

There are two men on the boat. You shiver in a blanket as the boat motors quietly toward the mouth of the bay. As you pass under the Golden Gate Bridge, the captain guns the engine. Wind blows past your face and a wake spools out behind you. By the time the sun rises, you are far out to sea, no land in sight.

THE END

To follow another path, turn to page 9.
To learn more about Alcatraz, turn to page 103.

Chapter 4

CAN THE MECHANIC FIX THIS?

You grew up on a farm. You and your younger brother and sisters worked on everything from tractors and cars to power tools and boilers. You can fix just about *anything*—and you can build anything, too. You and your family were poor but busy and happy.

It was a good life, but it was a hard life too. Everything had to go right in order to pay your bills and have enough to eat. And when the crops went bad two years in a row, things were definitely not going right. You didn't have enough corn to feed your livestock, much less sell. Bills added up, and your family was hungry.

Turn the page.

When the bank repossessed the farm, you moved to a one-bedroom apartment in the city. Your dad had a hard time finding a job. He died a year later—from shame, you always thought.

Finally, you found a job in an auto shop. You made good money, and it felt good to help pay for rent and groceries. But one day, things turned bad again. Two men came into the shop front; one of them had a gun. "Give me all the cash in the drawer," the other one said.

The men did not see you in the back office, but you saw them. It made you angry that these men would just take what they didn't earn. Meanwhile, your hardworking family starves. While your boss took the money out of the drawer, you hit the gunman in the arm. The gun fell to the floor, and you dove after it. So did the other two men.

After a brief fight, the gun went off. One of the men was shot and killed.

You were arrested and sent to trial for your involvement. The judge wanted to make an example of you. You were convicted and sent to Alcatraz.

Every day you think about your mom and siblings. It hurts you that you can't help them. If you could get out, you'd flee to another country and change your identity. You'd find a job and send money home to your family.

To take a job in the prison library, turn to page 76.
To take a job in the maintenance shop, turn to page 78.

Library workers get to push the cart of books and magazines around the cell block. You bring prisoners their reading material. Sometimes, you also pass secret messages. Working in the library is a good way to learn things.

It doesn't take long to notice that there are two brothers on the cell block who pass a lot of contraband back and forth. John and Jeff Bishop tuck the notes into different books that they take turns borrowing. Of course, you mind your own business.

One day at the end of your shift, a well-dressed guard asks you if you've seen any messages or other contraband on the job. His name is Lieutenant French.

"No, sir," you tell him.

"Well, keep an eye out," French says, winking.

The average prison sentence
at Alcatraz was eight years.

If you turn in someone who is passing notes,
you can earn privileges. You can even get time
taken off your sentence.

If you tell the guard about the Bishop brothers,
turn to page 80.

If you warn the brothers to be careful, turn to page 82.

You've spent your whole life fixing things. It only makes sense to take a job in the maintenance shop.

Working with you in the shop is another worker named John Bishop. Bishop has been in Alcatraz for a long time. He has a reputation for violence. He is dangerous and unpredictable. You mind your own business and try not to talk to him. But one day you notice him staring at you while you're repairing a hair clipper from the barbershop.

"What?" you say.

"You're good with machines," he says.

"Pretty good. Why?" You realize he has been watching you a lot lately. When he steps closer, you start to worry.

But instead of attacking you, he whispers, "Could you convert the motor in one of those electric razors?"

"Convert it into what?" you ask.

"A drill."

You can do this. It wouldn't be too hard—if you were on the outside. In here? Who knows.

To tell him you can do it, turn to page 84.
To keep minding your own business, turn to page 86.

For the next couple weeks, you track how many messages go back and forth between the Bishop brothers. You even find a razor blade in a book. The next time Lieutenant French asks, you detail how many notes are passing between them. You looked at one, and it was a map of the prison. French nods. He sits quietly for a moment, thinking, then gets on the phone and begins to dial a number.

"You can go," he says. Another guard escorts you back to your cell.

After dinner that night, you and the other prisoners return to the cell block. But something is going on. Jeff Bishop's cell, which is next to yours, is open. Lieutenant French, two other guards, and the warden are standing before it.

Bishop's bed and books are lying in a messy heap in the hall. One of the guards holds a sharpened spoon handle and a razor blade. The spoon handle could be a weapon or a digging tool—or both.

Bishop looks at you with cold eyes; he knows what you did. You realize you have made a terrible mistake. He and his brother will be punished—they'll go to solitary for many months for their foiled escape plan. But then they will return to the cell block. You will never be safe from them. Even if the warden is extremely generous about cutting down your sentence, you can't get out soon enough. You'll be dead.

THE END

To follow another path, turn to page 9.
To learn more about Alcatraz, turn to page 103.

The next day as you push the cart past John Bishop's cell, you pause. "French has heat on you," you whisper. Bishop nods slightly and goes back to his reading.

Days later, Jeff Bishop sits by you at dinner. His brother told him what you said. He thanks you. Then he lowers his voice and says, "We have a way out. But we need someone who can build and fix things."

You don't hesitate. "I'm in," you say.

He gives a small smile. Days later he sits with you at lunch again. "Can you make a raft?"

Out of things found in the prison? The next few days you think about it.

If John Bishop can steal enough raincoats from the supply closet in the maintenance shop, maybe you can make a raft.

The New Industries building was a two-story building. The laundry room was on the upper floor. Industrial work, such as sewing clothing or making shoes, took place downstairs.

But does French still have heat on the Bishop brothers? Maybe it's not safe to get involved.

To tell the boys you can make a raft, turn to page 88.

To keep your distance for now, turn to page 90.

"I can make just about anything," you boast.

A week later, John's brother Jeff slides a cloth bundle to you around the front of your cells. You pull it in and turn your light out to avoid detection as you unwrap the cloth. Inside it are the clippers. There's also a long, sharp drill bit.

Your breath catches. It's illegal to have this in your cell. If you're caught, it will be a world of punishment. But your breath is short for another reason too. Maybe you can escape!

That night, working with no light, you convert the motor. By splitting the power cord to your desk lamp, you rig an electrical arc into a homemade welding torch. Using that, you attach the bit to the motor.

You pass it back to Jeff. But when he sits next to you at lunch the next day, he has bad news.

"We need a bigger drill," he says.

Apparently, he can get out of his cell. Behind the cells, he can get to an air shaft with bars across the top. But the drill wasn't strong enough to get through them.

You think about it. A bigger drill could probably work. On the other hand, if you could get up there, you might be able to find another way through.

To suggest converting a vacuum motor to a drill, turn to page 93.

To ask if you can get up there to take a look, turn to page 95.

"Nah," you say, and walk away. You're not going to get involved in this, whatever it is.

"Suit yourself," he says.

Things are normal for a few months. Then one morning during roll call, something happens. From the end of the corridor, you hear Lieutenant French bark, "Again!"

You look down the cell block, but you can't tell what's going on. Soon it becomes clear though. Two prisoners are missing. One of them is Jeff Bishop, whose cell is right next to yours.

The warden comes. Everyone is locked up. Later you learn that both Bishop brothers have tunneled out of their cells. They are no longer on the island.

A view from a guard station. Cell Block B is on the left and Cell Block C is on the right.

You can't believe it. Everyone said The Rock could not be broken. But they did it. You are excited for them. But at the same time a feeling of despair fills your gut.

You could have been with them.

THE END

To follow another path, turn to page 9.
To learn more about Alcatraz, turn to page 103.

You let the brothers know your plan. John Bishop will need to steal as many raincoats as he can get. You will get to work mixing a strong glue in your sink.

The brothers teach you how to tunnel out of your cell through the air vent in the back, like they have done. The concrete is loose and rotten.

Over the next few weeks, John Bishop steals raincoats. When he goes in for his shift in the shop, he is not wearing one. While he's working, the guards on duty change. When he finishes his shift, he pulls out a raincoat and wears it back to his cell. The new guard assumes he wore it in.

At night, you sneak through your air vent into the corridor where the coats are hidden. There, you carefully cut them apart and glue the parts together to shape two long pontoons.

When you finish the raft, the brothers tell you they want to go—tonight. You have dug holes in your wall. You have a huge raft hidden in the corridor. Staying is risky.

But there is a good reason to wait. The raft is large and will take a lot of air to pump up. If you have to blow it up with your lungs, it could take an hour—maybe longer. With more time, you could fashion a pump out of something. Then you could pump up the raft and get out on the water faster. Once you're on the outside, every minute is precious.

To convince the brothers to wait, turn to page 97.
To take your chances tonight, turn to page 100.

The Bishop brothers agree to hold off—at least for a little while.

While working in the library, you learn that some inmates are planning to fight their way out of the prison. This is bad news. There is almost no chance they will succeed. And afterward, it's going to result in searches of the prison. The Bishop boys have weapons and tools in their cells, and no time to get rid of them. They have even dug tunnels.

They decide they have no choice but to try to get out during the riot.

The next morning, you step to the front of your cell for the morning head count. As Lietenant French walks past the cell of a con named Stinky, Stinky stabs him with something. French screams and crumples to the ground.

Suddenly the cell block is a frenzy of violence. Prisoners are attacking guards with homemade daggers. Stinky gets ahold of French's gun and starts to shoot. The guards on the second floor open fire.

Turn the page.

Prisoners who misbehaved could be sent to solitary confinement.

Gun smoke fills the air. The alarm is going off. Guards and inmates are lying on the floor bleeding. You follow Stinky through the kitchen to the trash burner. He has French's keys, and unlocks the door.

Outside, you begin to climb a chain link fence. Stinky is laughing. He thinks he's made it. Just then, gun fire erupts behind you. The fence shakes. You look at Stinky. He looks surprised that they got him. His legs slip, but his fingers stay curled in the fence.

You keep climbing. But a moment later bullets tear into your own back, and you fall.

THE END

To follow another path, turn to page 9.
To learn more about Alcatraz, turn to page 103.

"I saw vacuum motors going into the shop for repairs," you whisper to Jeff. "I need one."

Jeff tells you how to use a sharpened spoon handle to dig out your own vent. That way you can get into the maintenance corridor like he does.

It takes a couple weeks of digging at night, but you get through. When you do, the stolen vacuum motor is in the corridor waiting for you. Using the same method as before, you convert it into a drill.

When it's ready, Jeff slips out of his cell. Suddenly, there's a loud noise—a loud noise that sounds a lot like a vacuum cleaner.

Jeff turns off the motor, but it's too late. Everyone heard it. Guards are rushing onto the cell block. They find Jeff's hole, and they find Jeff crawling back into his cell.

Turn the page.

In 1962 prisoners attempted to escape by loosening the air vents in their cells. One of the tools used was a drill made with a vacuum cleaner motor.

It's over. Jeff wastes no time in telling the guards everything. As you are locked into solitary, you think of your mother. Once again, you have failed to help her.

THE END

To follow another path, turn to page 9.
To learn more about Alcatraz, turn to page 103.

"A bigger drill might be too loud," you say. "But maybe I can get through the bars another way. I just need to get up there and see."

Jeff gives you the drill bit. You use it to dig out the concrete around the air vent under the sink. In a couple weeks, you get the grate out.

You climb through the hole and up to the top of the cell block. Jeff shows you the air vent, and you shimmy up inside. You inspect the bars. You realize there are screws holding the circular grill in the shaft. You take the drill bit and dig into the concrete around the ring. It crumbles, just like the concrete around the air vent in your cell.

Soon you reach a screw behind the circular grill. Using the drill bit, you're able to hack at it until it breaks. You repeat the process on the other side.

Turn the page.

You climb back down. "I broke two of the screws," you tell Jeff. "There are two more—we can break those when we are ready to go."

"We need a raft if we want to get across the bay," Jeff says.

You have a plan for that too. "Tell John to steal as many raincoats as he can from the supply closet in the maintenance shop. Hide them in the corridor behind my cell."

Soon, a pile of raincoats grows behind your cell. Every night, you sneak back there and cut the raincoats apart. You mix a strong homemade glue in your sink. In time, you build a two-pontoon raft. What you need now is something to inflate it.

Go to page 97.

You and the Bishop brothers are talking in the yard. Seagulls cry overhead. Clouds move quickly past in the heavy wind.

"I have an idea," you say. You have been watching a couple men play guitar out of the corner of your eye. "I'm going to order an accordion."

"Those things sound terrible," Jeff Bishop says.

"That's not the point," you say.

You order the instrument and practice playing it each night after dinner. You want the guards to think you really love music. There's no other reason for ordering an accordion.

Then one night you turn out your lights and climb through your air vents. You carry the accordion with you. The two brothers drag the raft and the sheets from their bed.

Turn the page.

At the top of the air shaft in the ceiling, you use the drill bit to chip away the final two screws in the circular grill of bars. You push it out over the top, being careful not to let it clang on the roof. Then you use the sheets to climb down the side of the building.

At the beach, you quickly remove part of the bellows and convert the accordion into a pump. What little music the instrument makes as you pump is lost to the wind and waves. The raft quickly fills—first one pontoon, then the other.

Using bookshelves as paddles, you move easily across the bay. When you near the shore, you puncture the raft so it sinks. The authorities will find it and assume it sank with you on board. You hope they will think you drowned.

A view of the main cell block. In Alcatraz's 29-year history, 36 men were involved in 14 escape attempts. Two men tried to escape twice.

Your patience has paid off. With the head start you got, you will be far away before they even realize you're gone. You and the brothers split up. You hitchhike to Canada. When you get there, you'll get a job. As soon as you can, you'll start sending money home to your family.

THE END

To follow another path, turn to page 9.
To learn more about Alcatraz, turn to page 103.

That night, you and the Bishop brothers all break out through your loose ventilation grates. You climb to the top of the cell block and into the empty air shaft. You pull the bulky raft up behind you. Soon, you are all outside on the rooftop. The ocean air smells great! It smells like freedom.

You toss your raft over the side of the building. Using bedsheets from your cells, you climb down to the ground. The three of you drag the raft to the shore, where you take turns blowing into it. You were right—it takes a long time. Even after half an hour, it still looks flat.

Finally, you decide it's close enough. You push your flabby boat out into the waves and climb in. Using a bookshelf from your cell, you paddle out into the fog.

The raft begins taking on water. Even the smallest waves splash over the sagging sides.

You bail out as much as you can with your hands, but it's a losing battle. The raft is going slower and slower with the extra weight. And the water is over your knees as you kneel in the bottom. The brothers whisper among themselves. Then they turn to you.

"There's too much weight in here," John Bishop says.

They plan to throw you overboard. Instead of letting them, you jump out. It won't help them anyway. They might make it farther than you. But you're all going to end up at the bottom of the bay.

THE END

To follow another path, turn to page 9.
To learn more about Alcatraz, turn to page 103.

Chapter 5

THE ESCAPE-PROOF ROCK

The earliest known occupants of the island that came to be known as Alcatraz were indigenous peoples known as Ohlone. The Ohlone sent their criminals to live on the island in isolation.

In 1759 a Spanish explorer named Juan Manuel Diaz discovered the island and named it "La Isla de los Alcatraces," or "The Island of Pelicans." Apparently the island was home to many brown pelicans.

The Spanish built some buildings while they were there. The land passed to the United States after the Mexican-American War (1846–1848). They built a fortress and armed it during the Civil War (1861–1865).

The first prison wasn't built until 1867. Then the U.S. Department of Justice took over in 1933. It became a federal prison the following year.

Alcatraz Federal Prison was where the most dangerous criminals were sent. It housed such notorious men as Al Capone (known as "Scarface"), George Barnes ("Machine Gun Kelly"), Bumpy Johnson, and James "Whitey" Bulger. Its isolated island location, as well as the most modern high-security reinforcements, gave it the reputation of being considered escape-proof.

That reputation didn't stop prisoners from trying. During its 29 years as a federal penitentiary, there were 14 escape attempts. The official line is that none of them were successful. Not everyone agrees with that.

Alcatraz was closed as a prison on March 21, 1963. It was deemed too expensive to keep up. Later it reopened as a museum. Visitors can ride a boat to the island and tour the buildings and hear stories about life on The Rock.

In 1962 convicts used fake heads made with soap, toilet paper, paint, and real human hair to fool prison guards into thinking they were still in their cells.

REAL ESCAPE ATTEMPTS

April 27, 1936: A prisoner working at the garbage incinerator makes a run for it. He was shot trying to climb the fence.

December 16, 1937: Two prisoners filed through iron bars and got out. They are believed to have drowned in stormy waters.

May 23, 1938: Three men killed a guard with a hammer in the woodshop. Two were shot and killed, and the other man surrendered on the roof.

January 13, 1939: Five inmates escaped from their cells and made it to the shore. A guard spotted them and opened fire, killing one man and wounding another. The others were taken alive.

May 21, 1941: Four inmates took several guards hostage. But they could not saw through the tool-proof bars to escape before being re-captured.

September 15, 1941: An inmate slipped away from the guards while working on garbage duty. He started to swim for freedom but gave up.

April 14, 1943: Four inmates cut through the bars in an industrial room. They collected cans to use as flotation devices. They attacked and tied up two guards before escaping out the window. The guards managed to get loose and alert the prison. One prisoner was killed, two were recovered, and one remained missing. He hid in a nearby cave, but after two days snuck back in the same window he had escaped from.

August 7, 1943: An inmate working in the laundry escaped and made it to the two security fences. He had stolen wire cutters, but they didn't work, and he had to climb both fences. He fell from the second fence and injured his back. He was captured.

July 31, 1945: A prisoner stole an army uniform from the laundry and got on board a government boat. But when he was discovered to be missing through a headcount, the boat was held at Angel Island, where he was caught.

May 2—4, 1946: Six prisoners staged a violent riot, later named the Battle of Alcatraz. They attacked guards and got into the weapons room. There, they got keys to the recreation yard. But they ended up in a bloody fight. They took two guards hostage. The U.S. Marines were called in and helped the guards kill three of the convicts. The prisoners had already killed the two hostages and injured 17 other guards. The three surviving inmates who started the riot were convicted of murder, and two of them were sentenced to death. Clarence Carnes, who was only 19 years old, was given a second life sentence on top of the one he already was serving.

July 23, 1956: A prisoner escaped from his job at the dock. He hid in the rocks at the shore and tried to build a raft out of driftwood. He was soon caught.

September 29, 1958: Two convicts escaped while working on garbage detail. One was caught in the water. The other drowned, and his body was discovered two weeks later.

June 11, 1962: Frank Morris, John Anglin, and his brother Clarence Anglin had reputations of escaping prison. They worked together to escape. Each dug away the concrete surrounding their cell's air vents, gaining access to a utility corridor behind the wall. They made fake walls and grills out of paper-mache to hide their work.

They also made paper-mache heads to leave on their pillows. The heads made it look like they were still in their cells while they were outside building a raft.

Another convict, Alan West, tricked the guards into hanging sheets over the third-floor railing. He told them it was to keep dust from falling while he cleaned up there. Morris and the Anglins used the sheets to hide their raft.

On the night of their escape, West could not get out of his cell. His "door" was not ready, and the other three left him behind. They climbed to the top of the cell block and into an air vent that had had its fan removed. The men were never seen again.

A gangster named Bumpy Johnson was rumored to have arranged for a boat to pick them up. Years later, a photo surfaced of two men who looked a lot like the Anglin brothers. The men were in Brazil. But nothing ever came of it. To this day, many believe the men escaped. Alcatraz officials said they died crossing the bay. But nobody knows for sure.

December 16, 1962: Two prisoners slipped out a kitchen window and tried to swim to freedom. One was found on a small rocky island not far away. The other was discovered near the Golden Gate Bridge. He had hypothermia and was in shock. Both were returned to Alcatraz.

OTHER PATHS TO EXPLORE

◈ Everyone loves a good escape story. But the men on Alcatraz were violent criminals. Does that make it harder to root for them? Why or why not?

◈ Do you think any of the men who really attempted to escape from Alcatraz were successful? Why or why not?

◈ A successful escape from Alcatraz means getting out of your cell, out of the prison, across the bay, and far away from San Francisco. Make up your own escape story. How would you do each of these parts?

READ MORE

Braun, Eric. *Escape From Alcatraz: The Mystery of the Three Men Who Escaped From The Rock*. North Mankato, MN: Capstone Press, 2017.

Burling, Alexis. *Occupying Alcatraz: Native American Activists Demand Change*. Minneapolis: Essential Library, an imprint of Abdo Publishing, 2017.

Evans, Christine. *Escaping Alcatraz*. Mankato, MN: The Childs World, 2018.

INTERNET SITES

Alcatraz History.
https://www.alcatrazhistory.com

Federal Bureau of Prisons: Alcatraz.
https://www.bop.gov/about/history/alcatraz.jsp

National Parks Service: Alcatraz Island.
https://www.nps.gov/alca/learn/historyculture/us-penitentiary-alcatraz.htm

INDEX